teacher's friend publications

SUMMER!
idea book

a creative idea book
for the
elementary teacher

written and illustrated
by
Karen Sevaly

poems by
Margaret Bolz

Copyright © 1990, 2001
Teacher's Friend, a Scholastic Company.
All rights reserved.
Printed in China.

ISBN 0-439-49963-1

Table of Contents

This book is dedicated to teachers and children everywhere!

TF1604 Summer Idea Book

Notes:

Let's Make It!

TF1604 Summer Idea Book

Let's Make It!

Children are especially responsive to the various holidays and themes associated with the four seasons. With this in mind, Teacher's Friend has published the "Summer" Idea Book to assist teachers in motivating students.

WHO USES THIS BOOK:

Preschool and elementary teachers along with scout leaders, Sunday school teachers and parents all love the monthly and seasonal idea books. Each idea or craft can easily be adapted to fit a wide range of abilities and grade levels. Kindergartners can color and cut out the simple, bold patterns while older students love expanding these same patterns to a more complex format. Most of the ideas and activities are open-ended. Teachers may add their own curriculum appropriate for the grade level they teach. Young children may practice number, color or letter recognition while older students may like to drill multiplication facts or match homophones.

WHAT YOU'LL FIND IN THIS BOOK:

Teachers and parents will find a variety of crafts, activities, bulletin board ideas and patterns that complement the monthly holidays and seasonal themes. Children will be delighted with the booklet cover, bingo cards, nametags, mobiles, place cards, writing pages and game boards. There is also a special section devoted to the sport of the season!

HOW TO USE THIS BOOK:

Every page of this book may be duplicated for individual classroom use. Some pages are meant to be used as duplicating masters or student worksheets. Most of the crafts and patterns may be copied onto construction paper or printed on index paper. Children can then make the crafts by coloring them using crayons or colored markers and cutting them out. Many of the pages can be enlarged with an overhead or opaque projector. The patterns can then be used for door displays, bulletin boards or murals.

Making mobiles is especially fun for all ages. Teachers may like to simplify mobile construction for young children by using one of these ideas.

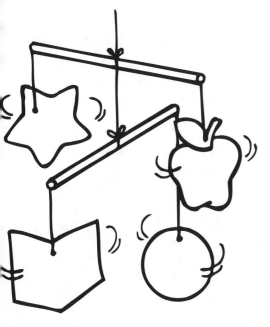

DRINKING STRAW MOBILE

Thread a piece of yarn through a plastic drinking straw and tie a mobile pattern to each end. Flatten a paper clip and bend it around the center of the straw for hanging. The mobile can easily be balanced by adjusting the yarn. (Older students can make their mobiles the same way but may wish to add additional levels by hanging other mobiles directly below the first.)

CLOTHES HANGER MOBILE

Mobiles can easily be made with a wire clothes hanger, as shown. Just tie each pattern piece to the hanger with thread, yarn or kite string.

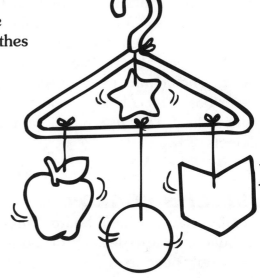

YARN MOBILE

Gluing the pattern pieces to a length of yarn makes the most simple mobile, each piece spaced directly beneath the other. Tie a bow at the top and hang in a window or from the ceiling.

CLIP ART PAGES:

The illustrations on these pages may be used in classroom bulletins, newsletters, notes home or just to decorate your own worksheets. Copy the clip art pages, cut out the illustrations you want, and paste them to your original before printing. The drawings may be enlarged or reduced on a copy machine. You are also free to enlarge the illustrations for other uses, such as bulletin boards, calendar decorations, booklet covers and awards.

PLACE CARDS OR NAMETAGS:

If possible, laminate the finished nametags or place cards after you have copied them onto colored index paper. Use a dry transfer marker or dark crayon to write each name on the laminated surface. After the special day, simply wipe off the names with a tissue for use at another time.

POETRY:

Children love simple, clever poetry. Use the poems in this book to inspire your students. You may want to have the students rewrite the poems for a timely record of their advancing handwriting skills.

Each morning, copy one or two lines, or an entire poem, on the class board. Ask the children to copy it in their best handwriting. Instruct them to write the date at the top of the page. Collect the poem pages and organize them chronologically in individual folders. This is a great way to show parents how their child's handwriting has improved throughout the year.

STAND-UP CHARACTERS:

All of the stand-up characters in this book can easily be made from construction or index paper. Children can add the color and cut them out. The characters can be used as table decorations, name cards or used in a puppet show. Several characters can also be joined at the hands, as shown. The characters can also be enlarged on poster board for a bulletin board display or reduced in size for use in a diorama or as finger puppets.

BULLETIN BOARDS:

Creating clever bulletin boards can be a fun experience for you and your students. Many of the bulletin board ideas in this book contain patterns that the students can make themselves. You simply need to cover the board with bright paper and display the appropriate heading. Students can make their own fish for a classroom ocean scene or creative writing ice cream cones for a hot weather display.

Many of the illustrations in this book can also be enlarged and displayed on a bulletin board. Use an overhead or opaque projector to do your enlargements. When you enlarge a character, think BIG! Figures three, four or even five feet tall can make a dramatic display. Use colored butcher paper for large displays eliminating the need to add color with markers or crayons.

WHATEVER YOU DO...

Have fun using the ideas in this book. Be creative! Develop your own ideas and adapt the patterns and crafts to fit your own curriculum. By using your imagination, you will be encouraging your students to be more creative. A creative classroom is a fun classroom! One that promotes an enthusiasm for learning!

SUMMER

SUMMER ACTIVITIES
SUMMER BULLETIN BOARDS
PICNIC BASKET
SUITCASE TRAVELS
PICTURE POSTCARDS
SUNDIAL
SUMMER MOBILE
SUMMERTIME CHARACTERS

SUMMER NEWS!
A NOTE HOME TO PARENTS!

SUMMERTIME ACTIVITIES!

SUMMERTIME

When every day is bright sunshine,
On a hammock, I'll recline.
A hammock strung between two trees
Rocked and tossed by gentle breeze.
Lying in the tree's cool shade
Sipping Mother's lemonade.
Lemonade will hit the spot
In the summer when it's hot.
But there are other things to do,
Swim and read to name a few.
Tennis, ping pong and croquet
Are perfect for a summer's day.

LEMONADE

A recipe for lemonade.
This is the way that it is made.
Measure one cup of each of these,
Sugar, water, juice you squeeze.
All of this you stir and mix.
Lemonade is fun to fix.
Add water now, one quart more,
Counting cups that would be four.
In hot weather, add to the mix,
Several ice cubes, five or six.

SUMMER COLLECTIONS

Encourage students to collect simple souvenirs from the various places they visit during the summer. Examples might be postcards, maps, placemats, brochures, etc. At the close of summer, children can make a collage of their collection and share it with the class as they give an oral report of their travels.

SUMMER MATH

Keep students up on math facts, even through the summer vacation, with this simple activity. Ask each student to bring in enough self-addressed, stamped envelopes for each week of the summer break. Once a week, during vacation, send one envelope to each child enclosing several practice math worksheets. Parents can become involved by checking the completed sheets. Students will improve their math skills and, at the same time, have the enjoyable experience of receiving mail from their teacher each week!

SUMMER BINGO!

This game offers an exciting way to introduce students to the summer season. Give each child a copy of the bingo words listed below or write the words on the chalkboard. Ask students to write any 24 words on his or her bingo card. Use the same directions you might use for regular bingo.

SUMMER BINGO WORDS

SUMMER	PICNIC	FAMILY	CAMPING
SUN	BAR-BE-QUE	VACATION	HIKING
HOT	HOTDOGS	TRAVEL	COOK-OUT
SHADE	WATERMELON	PLANE	CRAFTS
SWIMMING	LEMONADE	TRAIN	BOATING
DIVING	ICE CREAM	BOAT	FISHING
POOL	4TH OF JULY	AUTOMOBILE	LAKE
BATHING SUIT	FIREWORKS	POSTCARDS	RIVER
BEACH	PARADE	CAMERA	FATHER'S DAY
PARK	FLAG	PHOTOGRAPHS	GIFTS

Picture Postcards!

Copy the front and back of this product onto heavier paper. Draw your own vacation picture, write a note and mail it to a friend.

PLACE
STAMP
HERE

SUMMER BULLETIN BOARDS!

SPLASH INTO SUMMER!
Enlarge this cute swimming character on the class bulletin board to encourage summer reading.

List the titles of several books on strips of colored paper. Children might like to suggest their own favorite books and stories for the enjoyment of other students.

PICNIC GOODIES!
This picnic basket can be used in a variety of ways on the class bulletin board. Several baskets can be displayed, each with answers to math problems. The problems can be written on the picnic goodies. Students match the correct responses together.

The basket and goodies can also be used to display classroom monitors, reading groups, individual awards, or vocabulary words.

SUMMER TRAVELS!
Roadway strips of black paper, with dotted white lines, can be pinned on the class board for a motivating summer display.

Children cut automobile booklets from construction paper and write their own summer travel plans inside. Students might like to be creative and write about fantasy travels, as well!

Display the autos on the road-ways for a "moving" activity!

Splash Character!

TF1604 Summer Idea Book

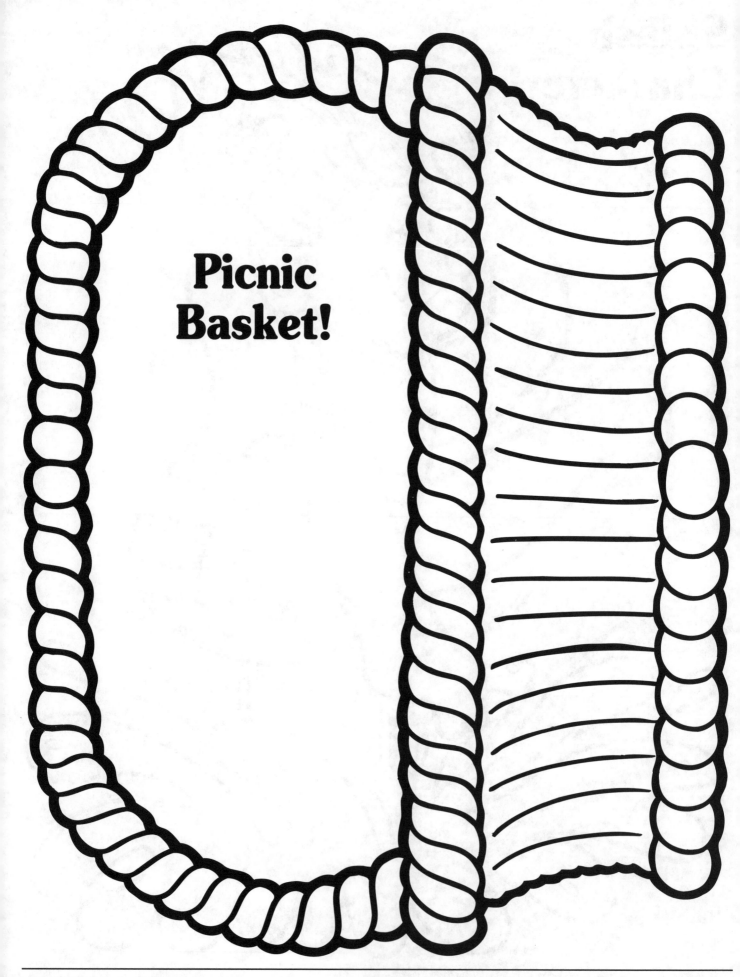

Picnic
Basket!

Picnic Goodies!

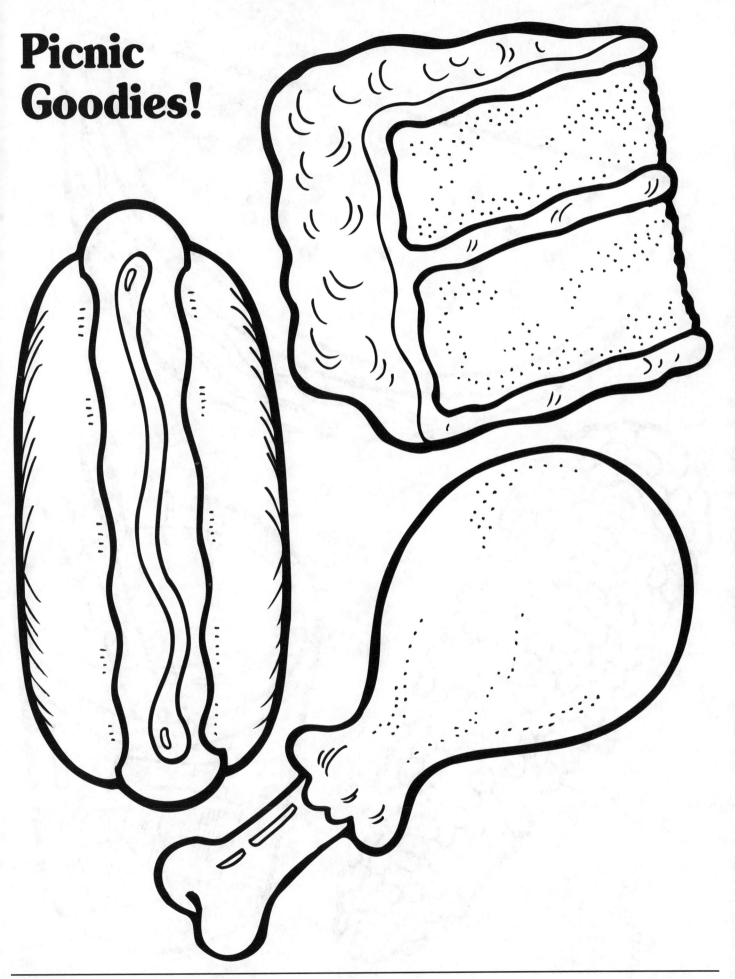

Summer Travels!

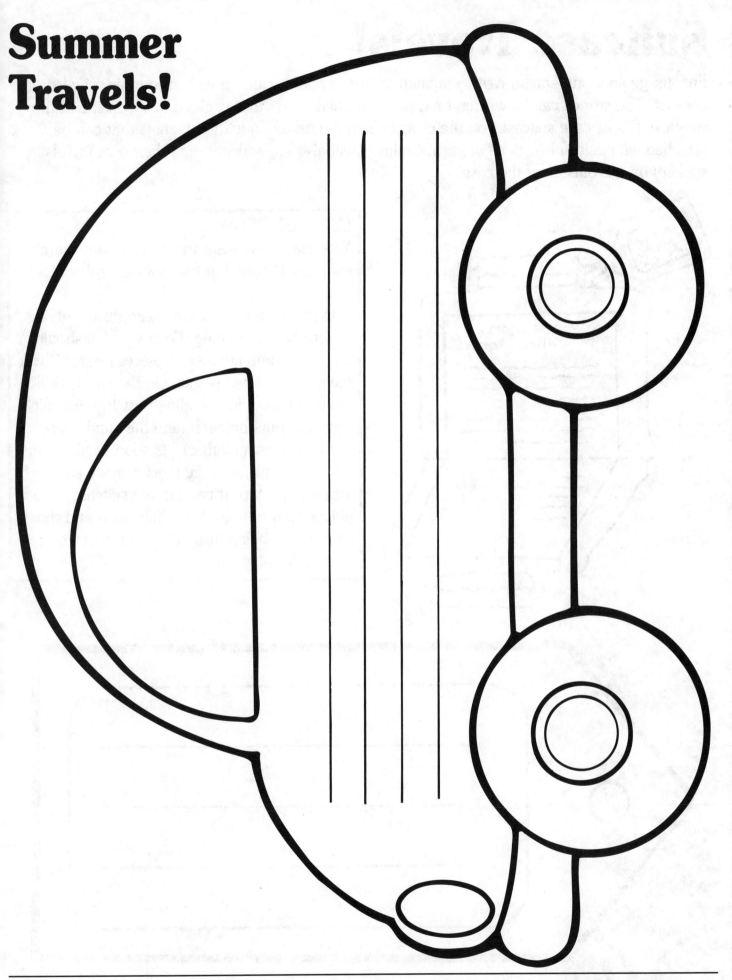

Suitcase Travels!

Encourage your students to write imaginative stories about exotic travels using this suitcase booklet. The stories can be written on a piece of lined paper that is glued to the inside of the suitcase. Display the suitcases on the class bulletin board along with nametags that can be attached with colorful sections of yarn. Children will also enjoy decorating their own travel stickers on the outside of the case.

SUITCASE RELAY

Your class may want to complete the exercise with this simple, but fun, suitcase relay race!

Bring two suitcases from home filled with a variety of old clothing. Each suitcase should have the same number of pieces inside. Divide the class into two teams. On the word "GO!" the first player in each line runs to their suitcase and puts on each item they find inside (over their own clothes). As soon as all of the clothing is put on, they must remove each article and place it back in the suitcase. The player then runs back to their team and the next player has a turn. The team that finishes first wins the game!

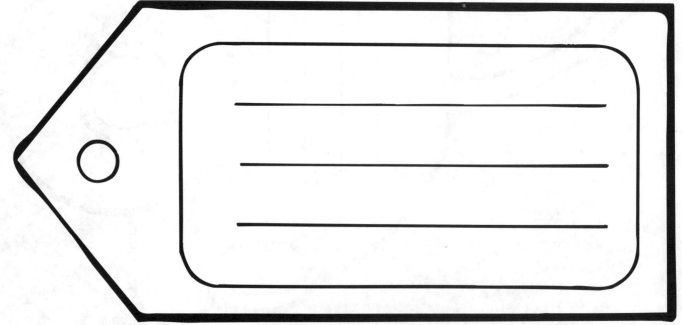

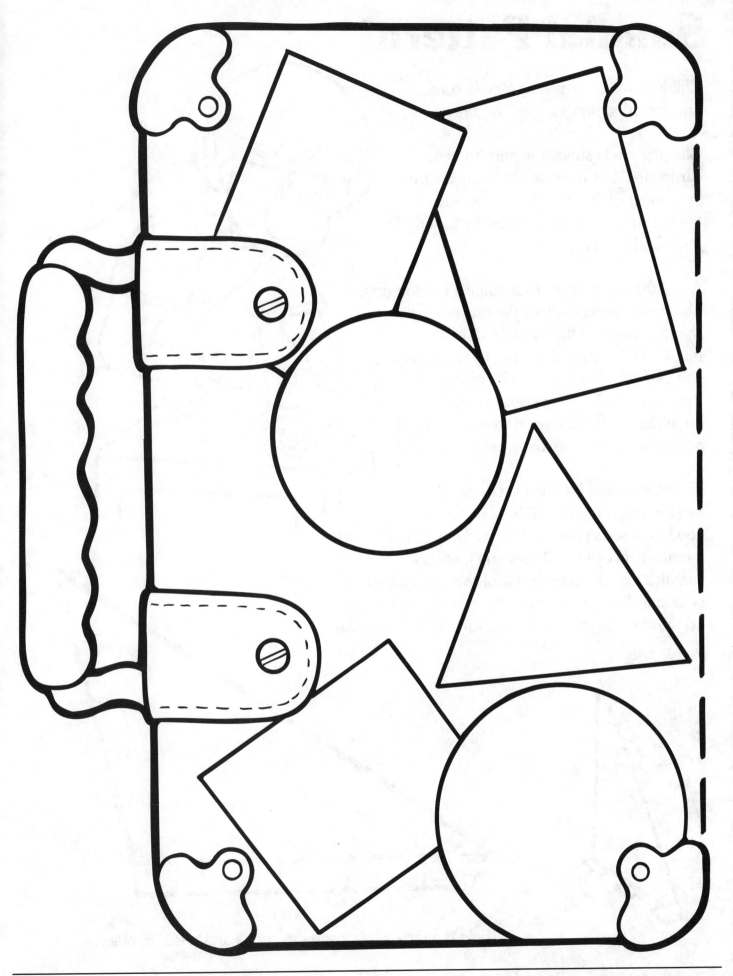

Sundial Pattern!

Children will love making simple sundials and recording the sundials' accuracy.

Glue the circle sundial pattern to heavy cardboard. Cut the triangle from construction paper or heavy index paper. Attach the triangle piece to the circle by pasting the folded tabs in place, as shown.

At 12:00 noon, place your sundial outside on a flat secure surface. Place the dial so that the shadow made by the sun falls directly across the "NOON" mark. Now, on any sunny day, you can tell what time it is by where the shadow falls. Check your sundial often during the afternoon to see if it is accurate to your classroom clock.

This sundial will be fairly accurate for most middle latitudes. This would be a good time to explain to your students the difference between longitudes and latitudes. You can also explain how the tilt of the Earth affects our seasonal changes and how this can also affect the accuracy of the sundial during various times of year.

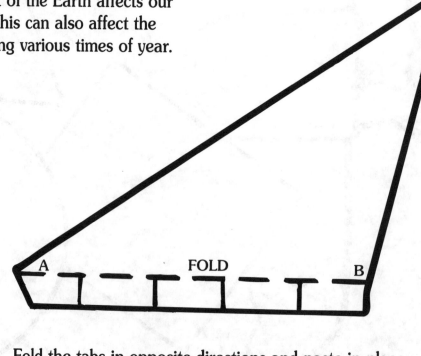

A   FOLD   B

Fold the tabs in opposite directions and paste in place.

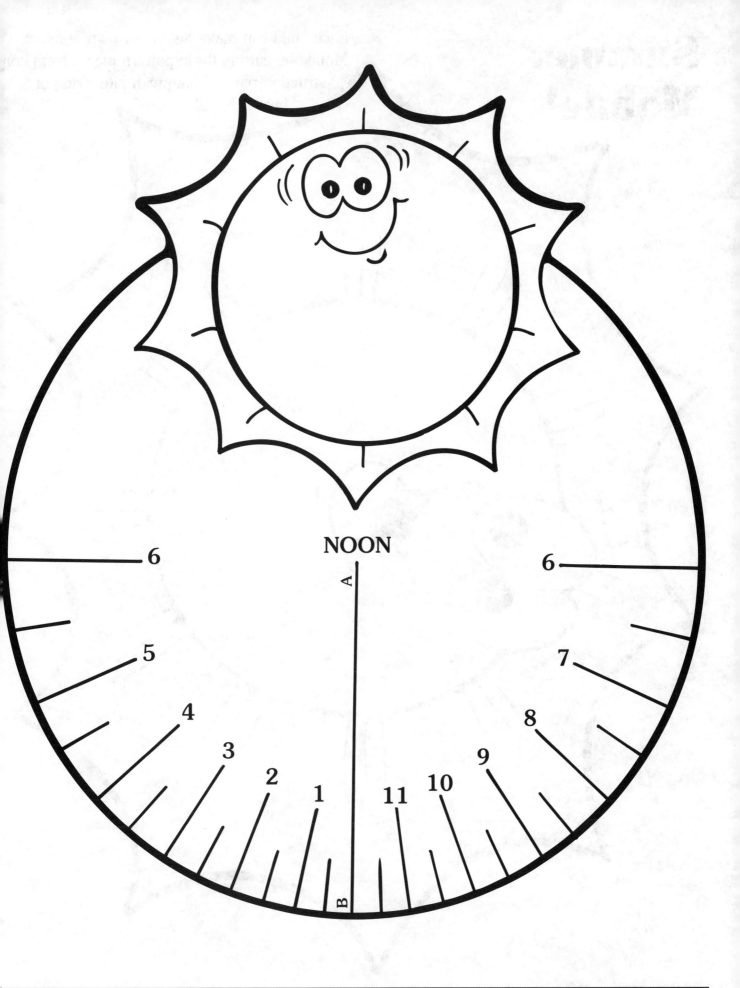

NOON

6

5

4

3

2

1

A

B

6

7

8

9

10

11

TF1604 Summer Idea Book

Summer Mobile!

Each child can make his or her own Summer Mobile by cutting these pattern pieces from construction paper. Hang with kite string or heavy thread.

TF1604 Summer Idea Book

Summertime Characters!

28

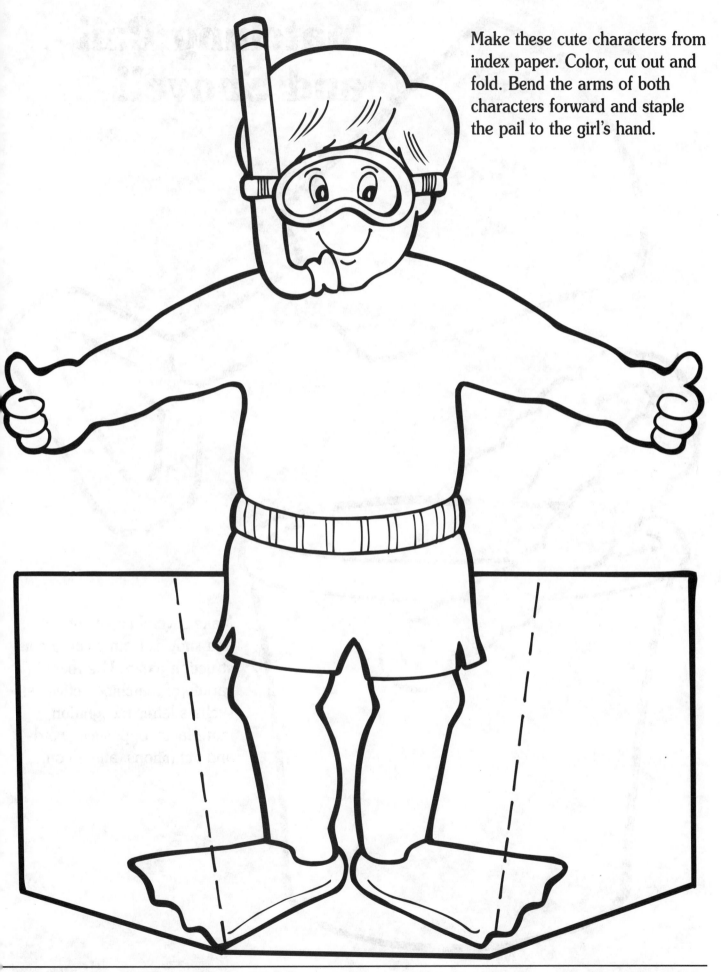

Make these cute characters from index paper. Color, cut out and fold. Bend the arms of both characters forward and staple the pail to the girl's hand.

TF1604 Summer Idea Book

Matching Pail and Shovel!

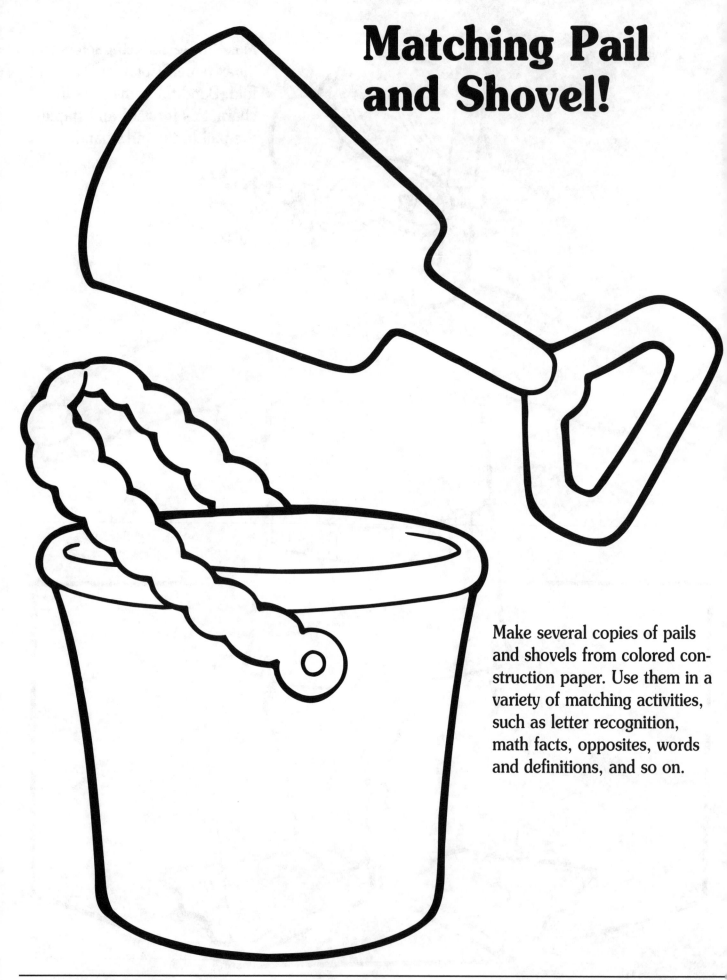

Make several copies of pails and shovels from colored construction paper. Use them in a variety of matching activities, such as letter recognition, math facts, opposites, words and definitions, and so on.

JUNE ACTIVITIES
JUNE AWARDS
JUNE CLIP ART
JUNE BULLETIN BOARDS
JUNE FUN GLASSES

"DEEP BLUE SEA" MOBILE
STAND-UP FISH
FATHER'S DAY ACTIVITIES
STAND-UP DAD
FATHER'S DAY COUPON BOOK

32

SUPER STUDENT AWARD!

awarded to

_____

for

_____

_____

_____

_____

Date

_____

Teacher

June

STUDENT OF THE MONTH

AWARDED TO

_____

Name

_____

_____   _____

Teacher   Date

JUNE NEWSLETTER!

TEACHER:	RM#	DATE:

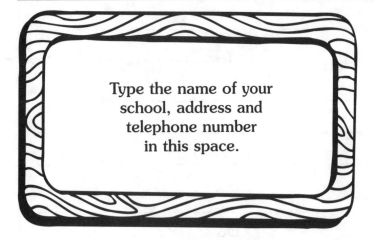

Type the name of your school, address and telephone number in this space.

SUGGESTIONS FOR A JUNE NEWSLETTER:

- List the name of each student that was selected student of the week for the month of May.

- Note the date of the last day of school, Flag Day and Father's Day. Make sure that parents know which days children will not be in attendance.

- List the dates and times of award ceremonies and celebrations that will be taking place those last few days of school.

- Tell about the special things your class has accomplished during the school year.

- Ask one of your students to draw several small pictures about Father's Day or the end of school to be used in the June newsletter.

- Ask your school principal to write a brief message that can be included with this year-end newsletter.

- Thank all of the parent volunteers that have helped in the classroom during the year.

- Announce any programs or special activities that children might like.

- List various local summer activities that parents and children would find enjoyable.

- Wish everyone a wonderful summer and make suggestions that might help parents reinforce good reading and study skills during the summer months.

June Clip Art!

TF1604 Summer Idea Book

JUNE ACTIVITIES!

THE MONTH OF JUNE

The month of June is quite unique,
With happy days in every week.
Good weather, weddings and vacations,
Flag Day, school's end, graduations.

Preceded by the month of May,
What's better than a bright June day?
The happy days will seem to fly
And then the month will be July.

What do you plan to do in June,
Marriage, wedding, honeymoon?
Diploma, graduation fun,
From college, high school or which one?

Display the flag, red, white and blue,
On the 14th, you should, will you?
The day in June I'm happy about
Will be the day that school is out!

YEAR END SCRAPBOOK

A fun way to remember each member of the class for years to come is with a scrapbook!

Assign each student their very own page to write you a note, include a poem, a drawing or add a photo. Make a cover from poster board and secure the book together with yarn or ribbon. Students will love being included in this special book!

WADING POOL READING

A small inflatable wading pool can provide a novel attraction for summer readers.

Place the empty pool in one corner of the classroom and encourage your students to use the pool during silent reading time.

WELCOME NEXT YEAR'S CLASS

This fun idea will give your students a chance to reflect on their many accomplishments during the school year and, at the same time, welcome the new class entering in September.

Ask each student to make his or her own "Welcome to Grade ____" booklet from the pattern provided. Different pages in the booklet can be titled, "My Favorite School Project," "Favorite Books I've Read," "My Favorite School Holiday," "My Tips for an Extra Good Year," etc. The last page of the booklet might contain a brief biography of the author. A photo or self portrait might also be included.

When the new class enters on the first day of school, surprise them with their own special "Welcome" booklet!

JUNE BULLETIN BOARDS!

PLANS FOR THE FUTURE

Children will love making their own self portraits donned in graduation caps and gowns. Students can then write about their plans and dreams for the future on scrolls of white paper. Pin the portraits and the scrolls, as shown in the illustration, for a thought provoking and motivating display.

SUNNY AWARDS

This motivational bulletin board will certainly put loads of sunshine into any classroom!

Display a large paper sun and several triangle rays on the class board. On the back of each ray, write a specific classroom award, such as "Extra 15 minutes at recess," or "Ice cream party on Friday!" When the entire class completes a required assignment, choose a student to turn over one of the rays to reveal the award!

DUNKIN' DOUGHNUTS

Children love doughnuts! Don't we all! Celebrate Doughnut Day on June 6th by having a class doughnut party. After the feast, children can use the doughnut booklet to write fantasy stories about doughnuts or creative recipes. Display them on the class bulletin board in this cute manner.

Doughnut Booklet

My Plans for the Future!

NAME

June Fun Glasses!

Cut the pattern pieces from heavy index paper and color with markers or crayons. Attach the bows to the frame by fitting them into the designated slots.

"Deep Blue Sea" Mobile!

Each child can make his or her own "Deep Blue Sea" mobile by cutting these pattern pieces from construction paper. Hang with kite string or heavy thread.

Amanda

Fillmore Fish

These sea creature patterns can also be used as bulletin board decorations or summer nametags.

Stevie Starfish

43

Christine Crab

Oscar Octopus

Stand-Up Fish!

Cut the fish and octopus from heavy paper. Write your own "fishy" message across the fish. Fan fold along the dotted lines. Glue the octopus to the first fish and stand on a desktop for a summer decoration.

FATHER'S DAY ACTIVITIES!

FATHER'S NAME

The children in Denmark
And in Mexico, too,
Call their father "papa"
Like the French children do.

It may be old fashioned
And a seldom used name,
But in dozens of countries
Today, it's the same.

With respect and with reverence
This title remains
Nearly all the world over,
Well known among names.

It's as well known as Father
And Daddy and Dad.
He's breadwinner, provider,
Good names he has had.

All over the earth
He's been known as Papa.
Revere him, endear him
And cheer him, Hurrah!

WONDERFUL DAD

Ask children to think of all the things that make their fathers wonderful. (Grandfathers, stepfathers, uncles or neighbors can always be substituted). Have them write their special thoughts on colored paper and include them in a Father's Day card.

STAR-SHAPED PAPER WEIGHTS

These easy Father's Day gifts are a joy to make and fun to give.

Grease the inside of a small star shaped cookie cutter with petroleum jelly. Place a cut-out photo of one of the children in the center of the cutter. Pour in a thick mixture of plaster of paris. When the plaster is dry, students can remove the paper weight and paint around the picture with yellow tempera paint. Cover with a coat of shellac for a glossy finish.

RECIPE FOR DAD

Children will love creating "Dad" recipes! Ask each child to write a recipe using the ingredients that make his or her dad special. Here is an example: In a large mixing bowl, combine 4 cups of security and 3 pounds of love. Briskly stir together with a tablespoon of generosity, a dash of patience, and a good measure of discipline. Bake it with warmth of kindness and serve it to all members of the family. What is this special treasure? My Dad!

Stand-Up Dad!

Make this Stand-Up Dad character from index or construction paper. Color, cut and fold. Attach the "Happy Father's Day" sign to his hands.

Stand him on a table for a Father's Day decoration or give him as a card to your dad on his special day!

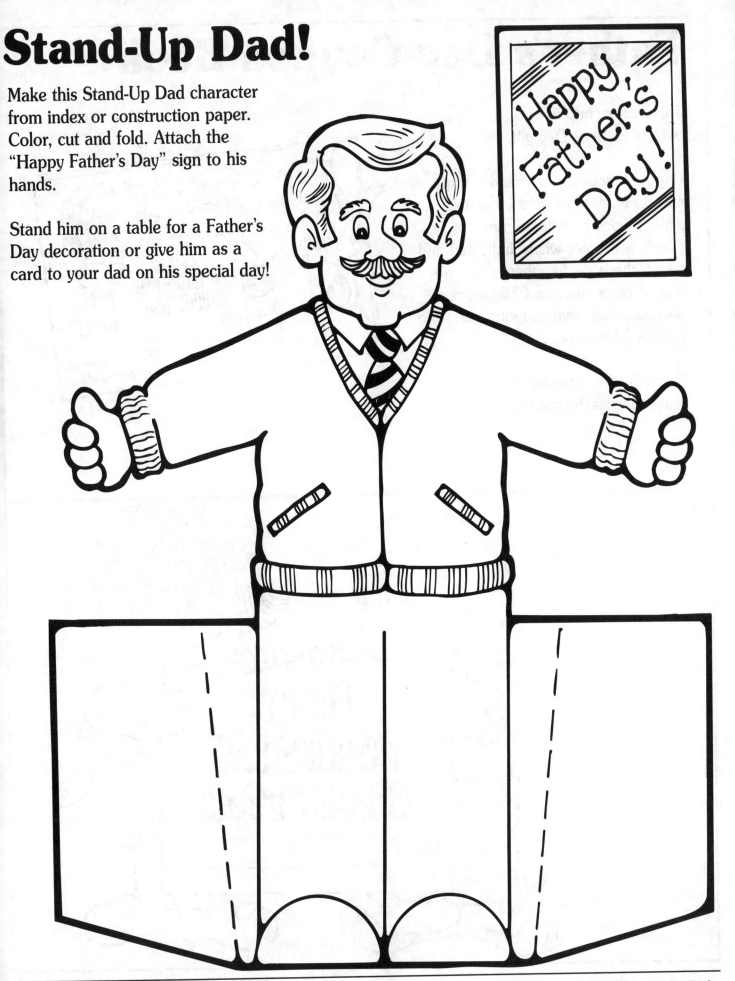

Father's Day Coupon Book

This clever coupon book makes a perfect Father's Day gift.

Copy the coupons onto index paper and have students do the coloring with crayons or colored markers. Punch two holes where indicated and attach the book together with a ribbon or piece of yarn. Children can also add their own coupons using the provided blank pages.

Dad will love receiving this gift and redeeming each coupon!

Father's Day Coupon Book

Redeem this coupon and I'll help clean_____

_____

_____!

Father's Day Coupon Book

Redeem this coupon and I'll feed our pets ___ times!

Father's Day Coupon Book

Redeem this coupon and I'll help in the kitchen _____ times!

Father's Day Coupon Book

Redeem this coupon and I'll help in the garden.

**Father's Day
Coupon Book**

**Father's Day
Coupon Book**

51

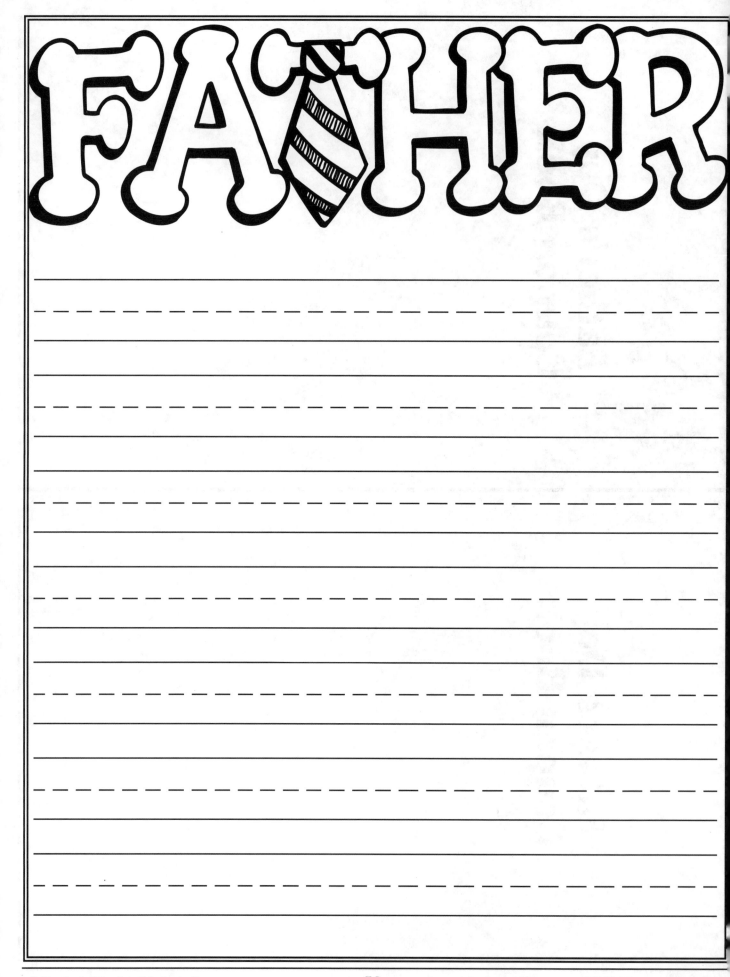

JULY AWARDS
JULY ACTIVITIES
JULY FUN GLASSES
JULY CLIP ART
JULY BULLETIN BOARDS
ICE CREAM MONITORS
UNCLE SAM CHARACTER
STATUE OF LIBERTY
STATUE OF LIBERTY CROWN AND TORCH
UNCLE SAM BEARD AND HAT
STAND-UP SHUTTLE
MOVABLE ASTRONAUT

SUPER STUDENT AWARD!

awarded to

_____

for

_____

_____

_____

Date

_____

Teacher

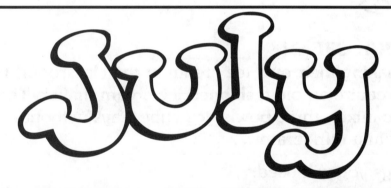

STUDENT OF THE MONTH

AWARDED TO

_____
Name

_____

_____   _____
Teacher   Date

JULY ACTIVITIES!

JULY

A flash of fireworks in the sky!
We celebrate Fourth of July.
We celebrate this glorious day
In bright and beautiful display.
It's summer, every day is hot.
Cool drinks and shade we need a lot.
Hot dog and mustard on a bun
Is my idea of picnic fun.
Is there any food you've known
That's cooler than an ice-cream cone?

MY SUMMER DIARY

Encourage students to write this summer by asking them to keep summer diaries. Have them write about things they get to do and places to go. Ask them to also write about events and activities that could have happened. They may want to include special jokes or riddles or even summer movie reviews.

STUDENT-MADE ICE CREAM

Children will love making their own ice cream in the classroom! Here's an easy recipe that doesn't require an old-fashioned ice cream maker. The only equipment needed is an electric mixer, three bowls, ice cube trays without dividers and use of the freezer space of any refrigerator.

For every 12 servings you will need:

2 cups of milk	1 tablespoon of vanilla
4 eggs	2 cups of whipping cream
1 cup of honey	2 ripe bananas

Beat the eggs in a large bowl adding the milk slowly. Continue to beat as you add the honey and vanilla. Mash the banana to add to the mixture. In a separate bowl, beat the whipping cream until it forms soft peaks. Fold the whipping cream into the egg and banana mixture. Pour into ice cube trays and partially freeze (about 2 hours). Return the frozen mixture to a large bowl and beat once again with the mixer. Serve right away in small paper cups and enjoy!

(If your ice cream becomes too slushy, simply place it back into the freezer for a few minutes before serving).

JULY NEWSLETTER!

TEACHER: **RM#**   **DATE:**

Type the name of your
school, address and
telephone number
in this space.

SUGGESTIONS FOR A JULY NEWSLETTER:

- If your school is still in session, list the name of each student that was selected student of the week for the month of June.

- Note the dates for Independence Day. Make sure that parents know which days children will not be in attendance.

- Announce special programs being conducted by your school or in your classroom.

- Ask one of your students to draw several small pictures about summer and the 4th of July to be used in the July newsletter.

- If your school is not in session during the summer months, you might like to mail a newsletter home to parents. This will require more time and organization, but it could be a real boost to each child's education at home.

- Include some math activities or work sheets with the newsletter. A reading list might also be included.

- List several safety precautions that should be observed during the summer months.

- Tell the parents and students about your vacation plans.

- Encourage parents to take their child to the public library or local museum.

- Include a summer calendar noting creative activities that children might do each day of the vacation.

July Fun Glasses!

Cut the pattern pieces from heavy
index paper and color with markers
or crayons.

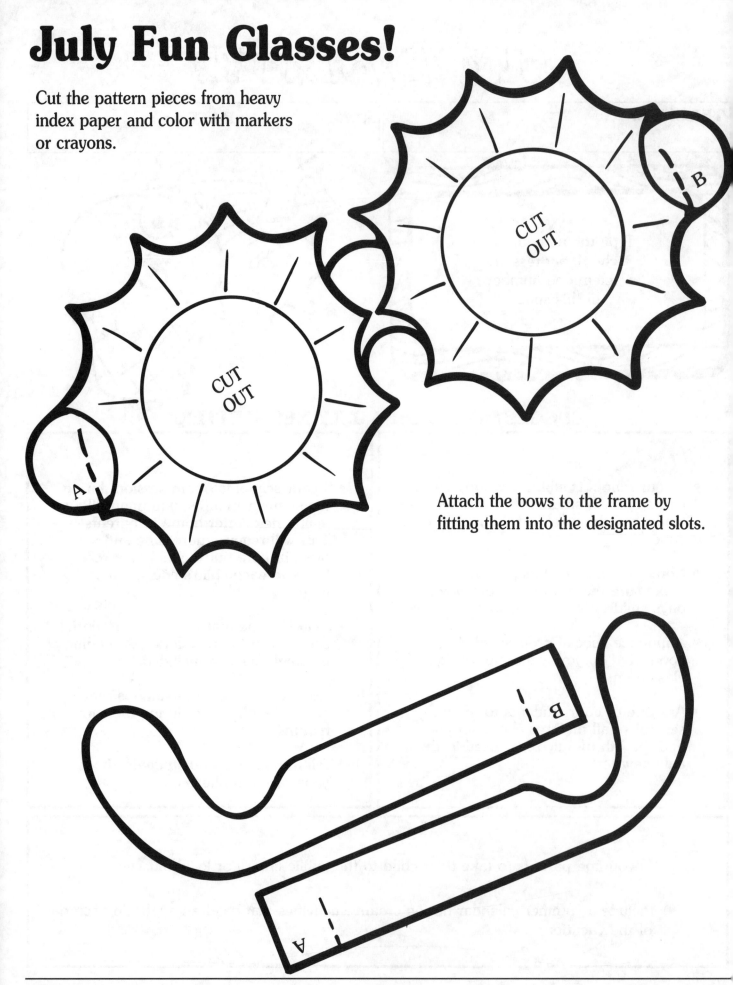

Attach the bows to the frame by
fitting them into the designated slots.

July Clip Art!

TF1604 Summer Idea Book

JULY BULLETIN BOARDS!

GET THE SCOOP!

This huge ice cream sundae provides a "delicious" way to encourage classroom participation.

Represent each child with a big paper scoop of ice cream on the class board. Students can add glitter "candy sprinkles," cotton "whipped cream," and red paper "cherries" to the class sundae when particular accomplishments are reached.

COOL RULES!

This extra large, multi-decked ice cream cone offers an excellent way to remind students of classroom rules or procedures.

Encourage the appropriate behavior by labeling the display, "Cool Rules." Schedule a class ice cream party as students' behavior improves.

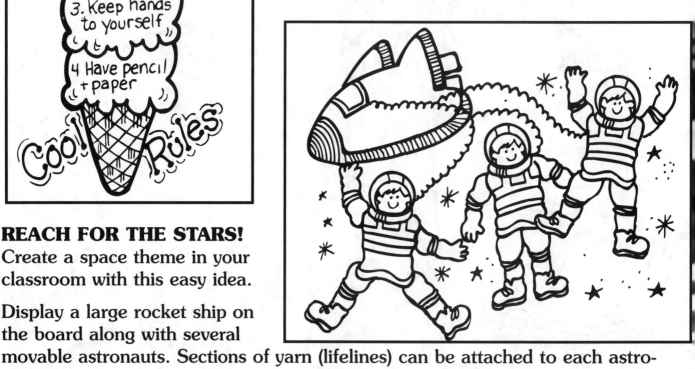

REACH FOR THE STARS!

Create a space theme in your classroom with this easy idea.

Display a large rocket ship on the board along with several movable astronauts. Sections of yarn (lifelines) can be attached to each astronaut.

Children can decorate the background with drawings of stars and planets.

Ice Cream Monitors!

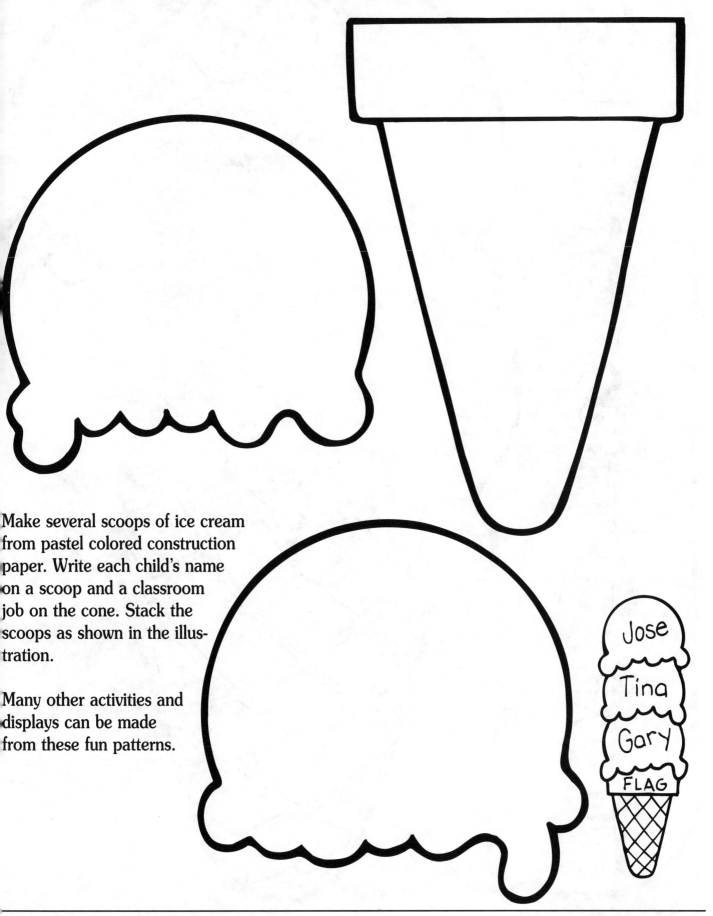

Make several scoops of ice cream from pastel colored construction paper. Write each child's name on a scoop and a classroom job on the cone. Stack the scoops as shown in the illustration.

Many other activities and displays can be made from these fun patterns.

Jose
Tina
Gary
FLAG

         TF1604 Summer Idea Book

MY ICE CREAM BOOK

The Flag of the United States of America

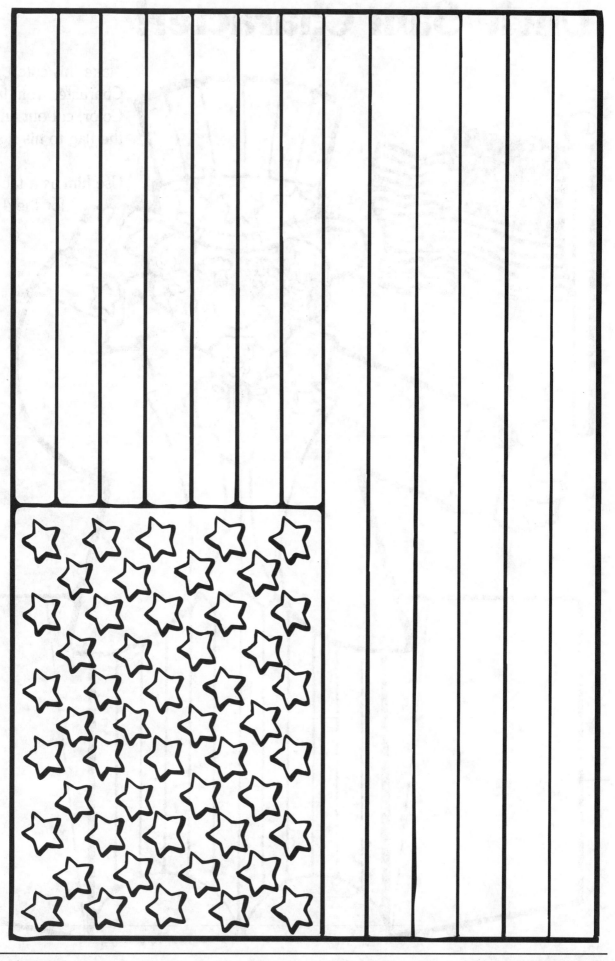

TF1604 Summer Idea Book

Uncle Sam Character!

Make this cute Uncle Sam Character from index paper. Color, cut out and fold. Attach the flag to his right hand.

Use him as a table decoration for the 4th of July!

Statue of Liberty!

This cute Statue of Liberty can be made from heavy index paper. Color, cut out and fold to make her stand on a table. Secure the torch to her right hand.

Statue of Liberty Crown!

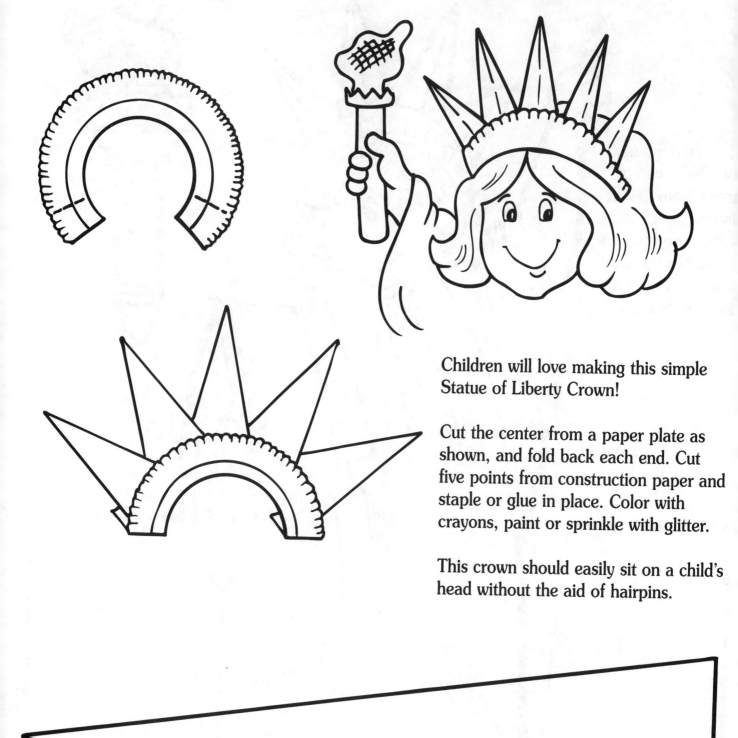

Children will love making this simple Statue of Liberty Crown!

Cut the center from a paper plate as shown, and fold back each end. Cut five points from construction paper and staple or glue in place. Color with crayons, paint or sprinkle with glitter.

This crown should easily sit on a child's head without the aid of hairpins.

TF1604 Summer Idea Book

Liberty Torch Pattern!

Color the torch patterns and cut them from heavy paper. Assemble them as shown. Use a cardboard tube from a used roll of paper towels for the handle of the torch.

1. Place the tube or handle of the torch through the center hole of the pattern. Fold the edges upward to form the base of the torch.

2. Fold the bottom of the flame in opposite directions and place in the tube. You may wish to tape or glue it in place.

TF1604 Summer Idea Book

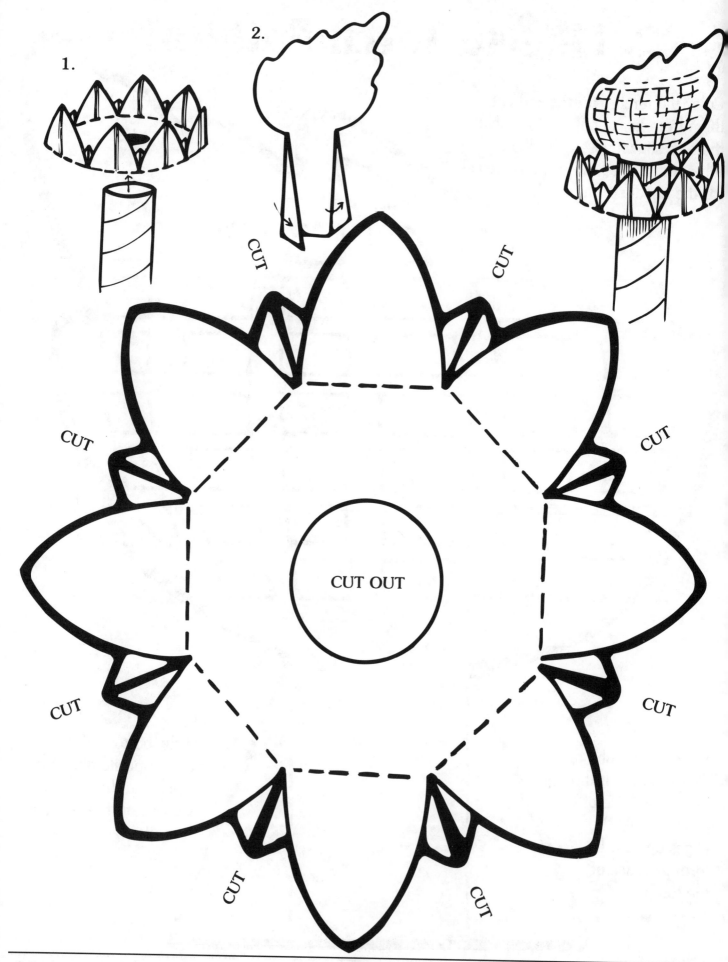

1.

2.

CUT

CUT

CUT

CUT

CUT

CUT

CUT

CUT

CUT OUT

Uncle Sam Beard Pattern!

Cut this Uncle Sam beard pattern from heavy white paper. Curl the ends of the beard around your ears to hold it in place. Wear it with the Uncle Sam Hat!

Uncle Sam Hat!

Cut this Uncle Sam Hat from white
construction paper. Color with crayons.
Staple the hat to a strip of paper
the correct size to fit the
child's head.

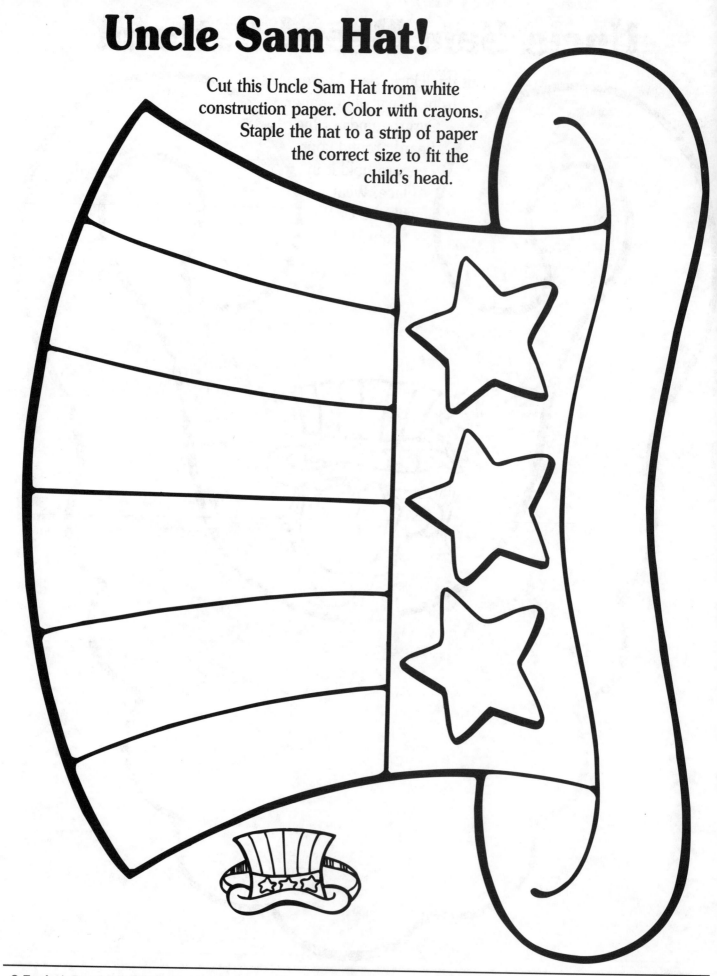

Stand-Up Shuttle!

Cut the space shuttle and cloud from heavy paper. Write your own "Out-of-This-World" message across the cloud. Fold along the dotted line. Glue the shuttle to the cloud and stand on a desktop as a decoration.

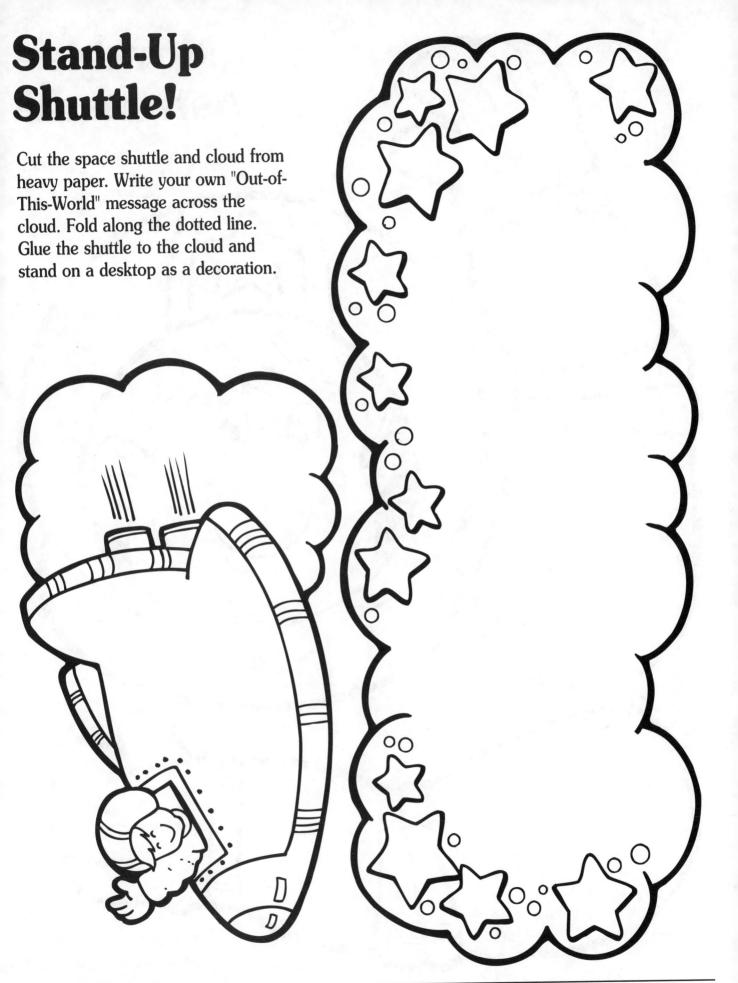

Movable Astronaut!

TF1604 Summer Idea Book

Cut this cute astronaut from colored paper and color with crayons or markers. Use brass fasteners to assemble at the dots.

Teachers might like to award a pattern piece of the astronaut for good behavior or completed assignments. Children can assemble the pieces together when they have collected all six.

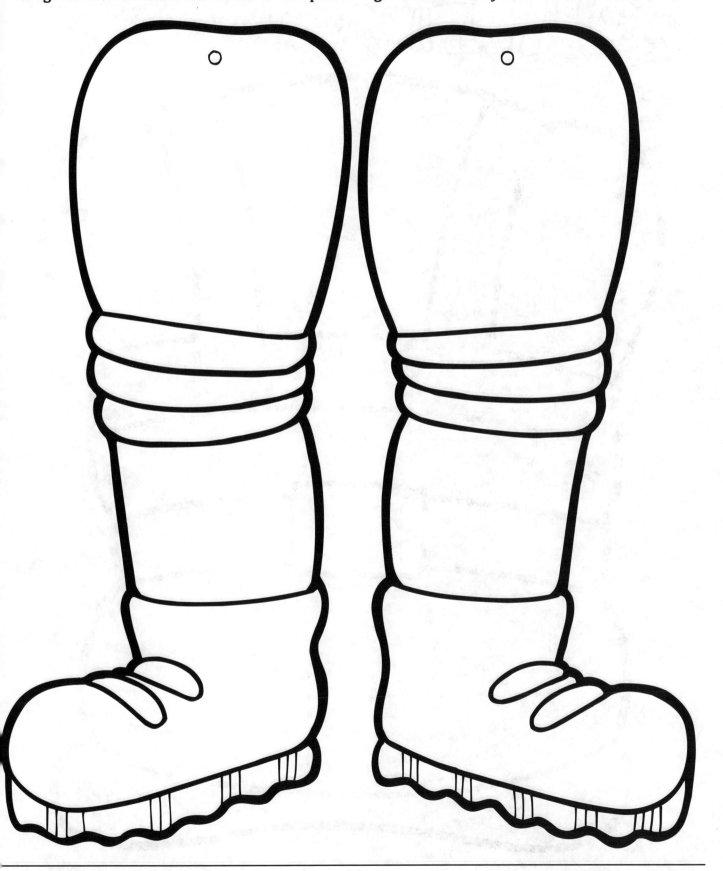

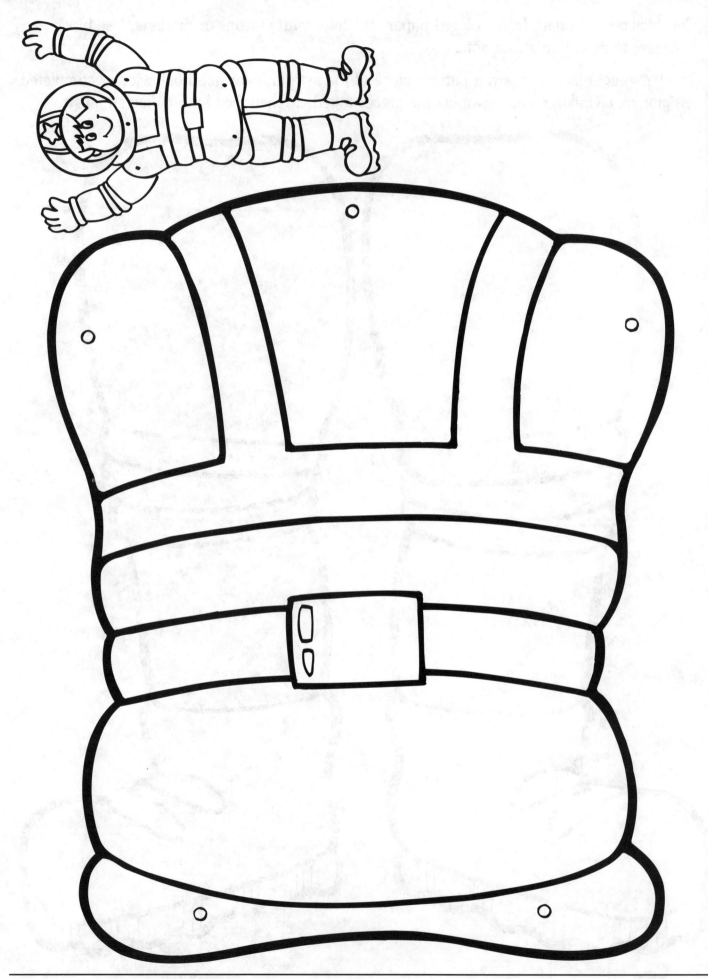

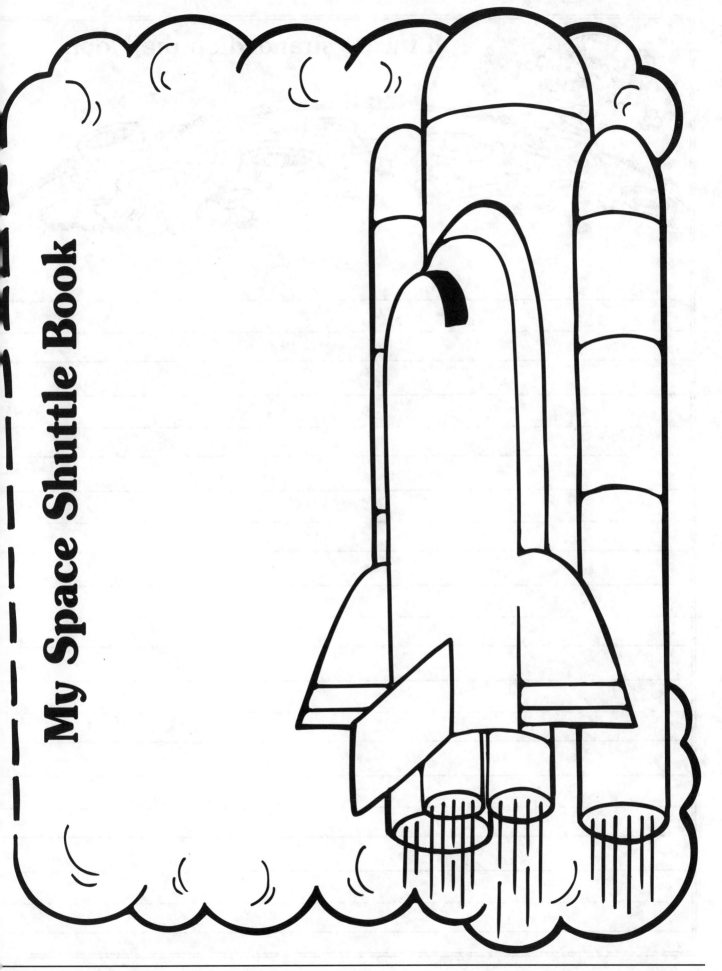

My Space Shuttle Book

TF1604 Summer Idea Book

If I were stranded on the Moon...

SUPER STUDENT AWARD!

awarded to

_____

for

_____

_____

_____

Date

_____

Teacher

August

STUDENT OF THE MONTH

AWARDED TO

_____

Name

_____

_____   _____

Teacher   Date

AUGUST ACTIVITIES!

AUGUST

August is a summer month.
The temperatures go soaring.
No holidays are in this month,
It may be somewhat boring.

The weather's always very hot
And every day with sun.
August is a longer month,
days add to thirty-one.

THE ENDLESS SUMMER VACATION!

This simple exercise will help even reluctant students look forward to the new school year!

Ask them their thoughts on what would happen if school stayed permanently closed and summer took over the entire 12 months of the year. At first, you may hear delightful shouts of joy, but after a few moments of thought, students will begin to conclude that an endless summer might not be as much fun as they thought. Have them write a few paragraphs about their feelings.

WHAT I DIDN'T DO ON MY SUMMER VACATION

Children will love having this new twist on the old creative writing idea about summer vacations!

Ask them each to think of things they wish they could have done over the summer, such as a trip to Disneyland or scuba diving lessons. They should also think of things that they are glad they didn't have to do, such as homework or shoveling snow!

Have them put their thoughts down on paper and display them on the class board.

ICE CUBE INVENTIONS

During the hottest part of summer, give your students a project that will really cool them off.

At the close of the day, announce the following assignment: "Tomorrow, you are each to bring an ice cube from home." A brief discussion might follow as how this feat might be accomplished without melting. But, don't give your students too many ideas. You'll be surprised in the morning to find a wide variety of containers, hand-made and commercial.

Students can judge the effectiveness of each container and award prizes to those that provided the best insulated containers. You might also like to recognize those with the greatest imagination and/or the person with the smallest successful container.

What I Didn't Do On My
Summer Vacation!

AUGUST NEWSLETTER!

TEACHER: **RM#**   **DATE:**

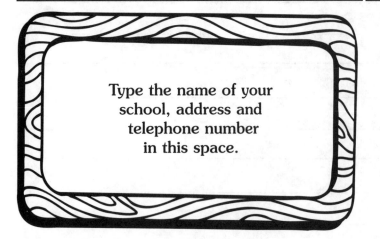

Type the name of your
school, address and
telephone number
in this space.

SUGGESTIONS FOR AN AUGUST NEWSLETTER:

- If your school has not been in session during the summer months, you might like to send your students some reminders and suggestions regarding the first few days of school.

- Note the date of the first day and remind them of the time school begins.

- Tell the students and the parents about some of the fun things you have planned for them for the coming school year.

- List the supplies and materials that you expect students to have on hand the first day of school.

- Provide a reading list and ask children to read at least one book from the list prior to the start of school.

- Describe the award program that you will be implementing in the classroom.

- List the classroom rules and homework policy. Emphasize the good behavior and happy attitude you expect from each student.

- Express your joy in having them in your classroom. Make sure that you emphasize how exciting and rewarding you expect the new school year to be. With this in mind, each student will look forward with happy anticipation to the first day of school.

August Clip Art!

TF1604 Summer Idea Book

AUGUST BULLETIN BOARDS!

WATERMELON DAYS!

This delightful bulletin board will motivate students even through the hottest of summer months!

Display a large, construction paper slice of watermelon for each student in class. As the children complete required projects or improve behavior, reward them with paper or real watermelon seeds. When each student has earned a predetermined number of seeds, celebrate by having a watermelon party!

LOOK WHO'S SPROUTING!

This extra large slice of watermelon is the perfect setting for encouraging students in classroom teamwork. Write each child's name on a black paper watermelon seed with white correction fluid and pin the seeds to the melon slice.

This is also a cute way to welcome students back to school if your school begins in the month of August!

PUT YOUR BEST FOOT FORWARD!

Display good work papers with this effective but easy bulletin board idea. Cut several footprints from colored paper and post them next to each good work paper. Students could also earn stickers or stars and attach them to their footprint!

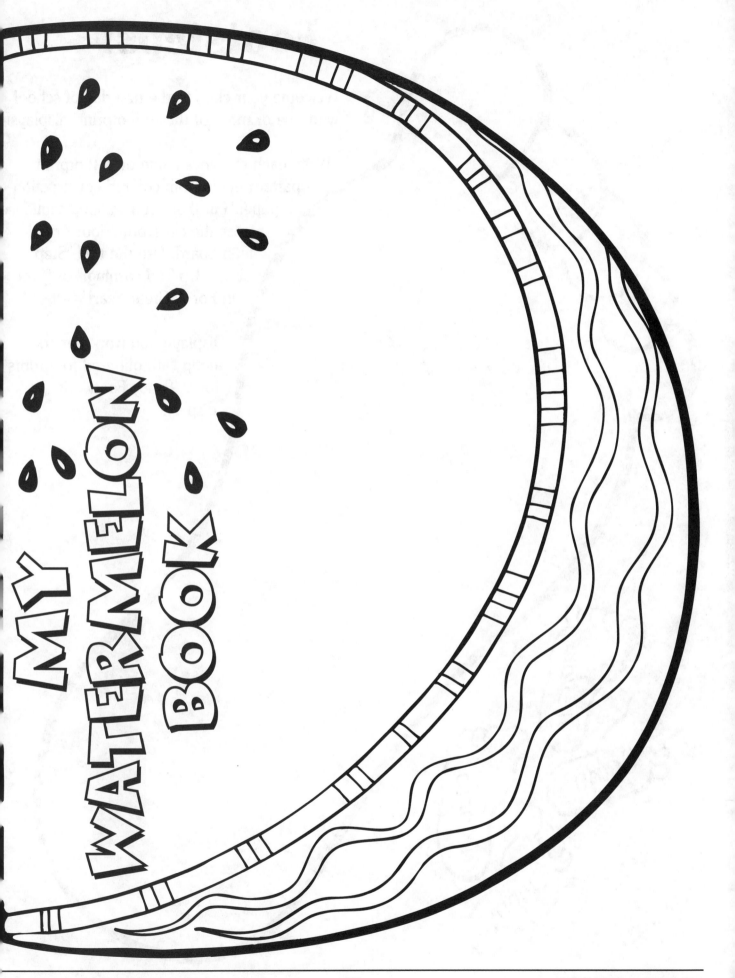

MY WATERMELON BOOK

TF1604 Summer Idea Book

Footsteps!

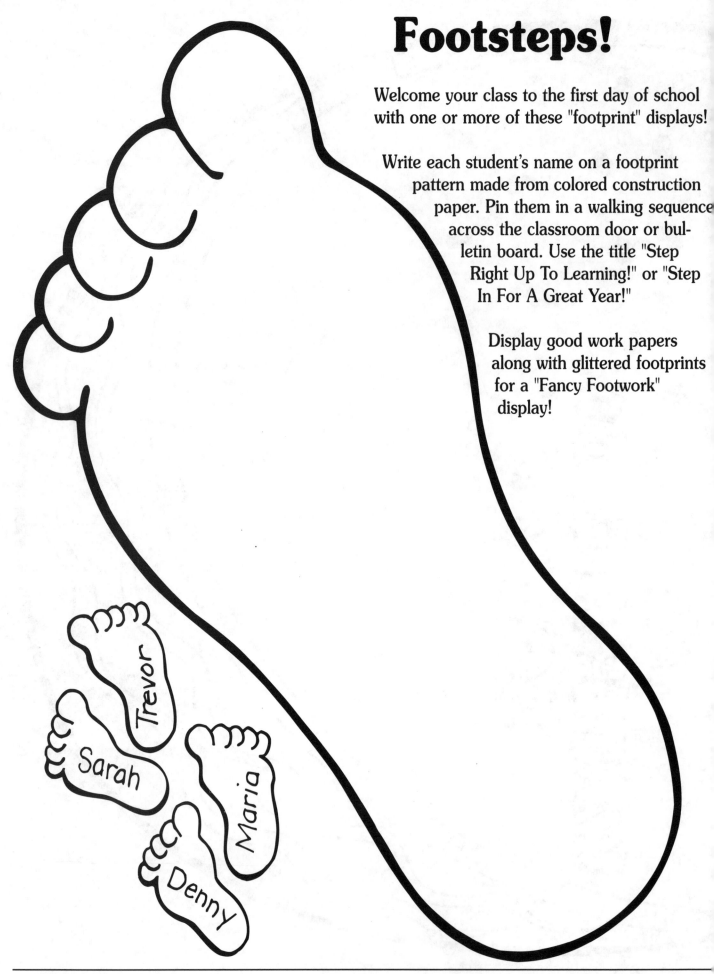

Welcome your class to the first day of school with one or more of these "footprint" displays!

Write each student's name on a footprint pattern made from colored construction paper. Pin them in a walking sequence across the classroom door or bulletin board. Use the title "Step Right Up To Learning!" or "Step In For A Great Year!"

Display good work papers along with glittered footprints for a "Fancy Footwork" display!

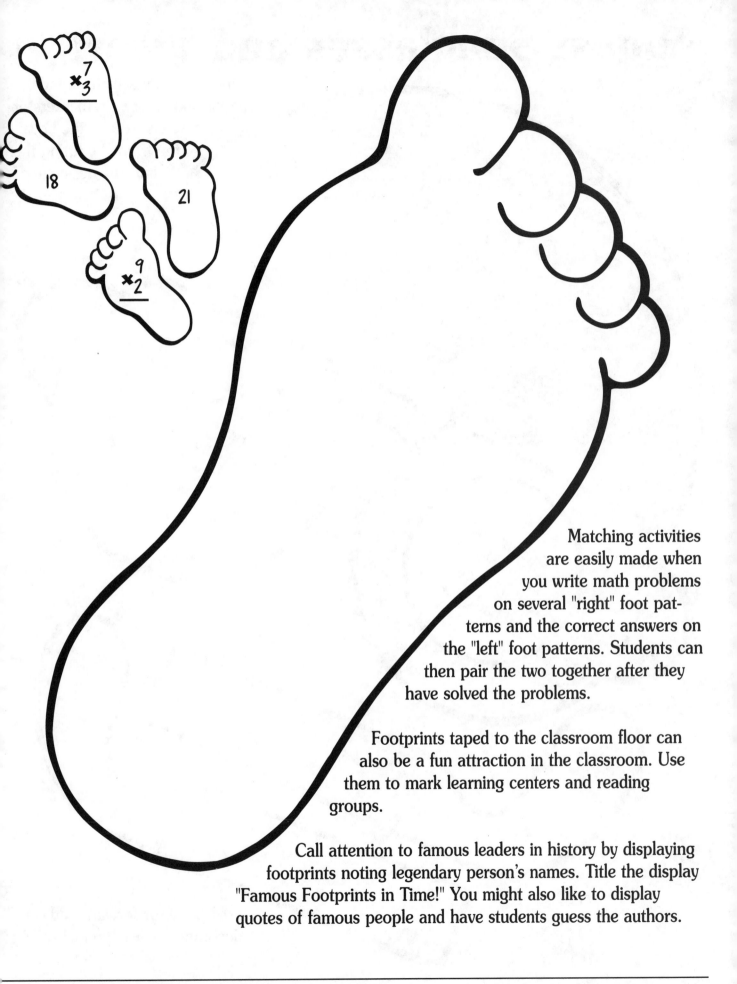

Matching activities are easily made when you write math problems on several "right" foot patterns and the correct answers on the "left" foot patterns. Students can then pair the two together after they have solved the problems.

Footprints taped to the classroom floor can also be a fun attraction in the classroom. Use them to mark learning centers and reading groups.

Call attention to famous leaders in history by displaying footprints noting legendary person's names. Title the display "Famous Footprints in Time!" You might also like to display quotes of famous people and have students guess the authors.

August Sunglasses and Visor!

Cut the pattern pieces from index paper and color with markers or crayons. Attach the bows to the frame by fitting them into the designated slots.

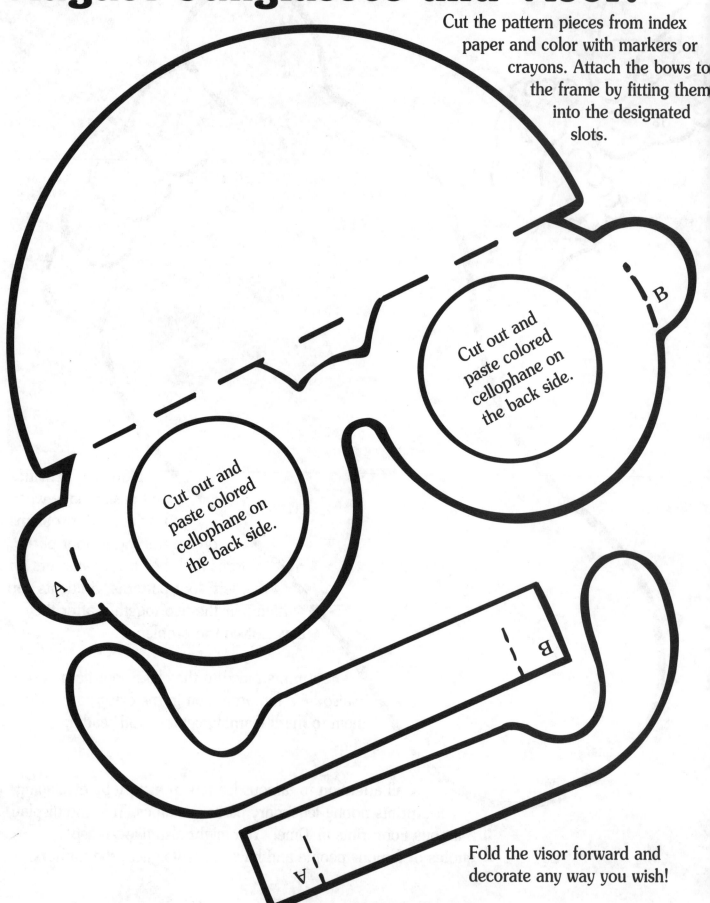

Cut out and paste colored cellophane on the back side.

Cut out and paste colored cellophane on the back side.

Fold the visor forward and decorate any way you wish!

Stand-Up Stars!

Cut the stars and pencil character from heavy paper. Write your own name or message across the stars. Fan fold along the dotted lines. Glue the pencil to the first star and stand on a desktop as a name plate or back to school decoration.

Taylor Kim Brian

CLEAN UP GAME BOARD

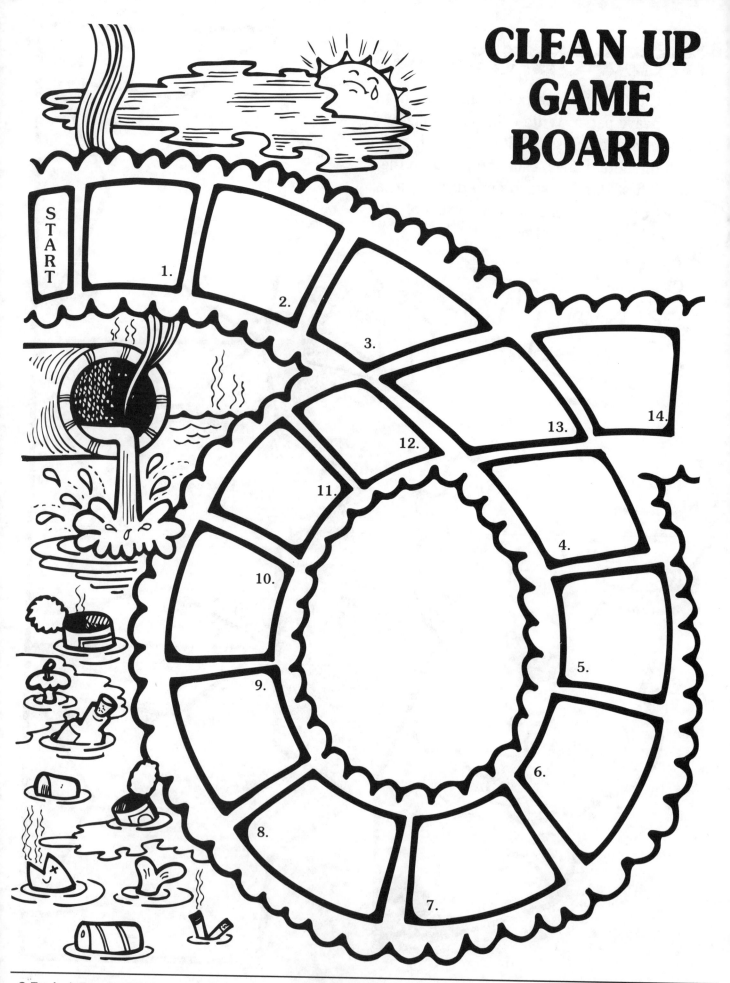

START

1.
2.
3.
4.
5.
6.
7.
8.
9.
10.
11.
12.
13.
14.

TF1604 Summer Idea Book

Use the task cards provided or make your own for this game that two, three or four children can play.

YOU PLANTED A TREE TO CELEBRATE ARBOR DAY! MOVE AHEAD 1 SPACE

YOU SAVED WATER BY NOT HOSING OFF YOUR WALKWAYS OR DRIVEWAY! GO AHEAD 1 SPACE

YOU ORGANIZE A NEIGHBORHOOD CLEAN-UP CAMPAIGN! MOVE AHEAD 2 SPACES

YOU RECYCLED ALL OF YOUR PLASTIC, GLASS AND PAPER! MOVE AHEAD 3 SPACES

YOU CONTRIBUTE TO AN ENVIRON-MENTAL GROUP THAT HELPS PASS LAWS TO CONTROL POLLUTERS! MOVE AHEAD 3 SPACES

YOU JOINED A CAR POOL! MOVE AHEAD 2 SPACES

YOU HELPED CLEAN UP GRAFFITI AT YOUR NEIGHBOR-HOOD SCHOOL! TAKE ANOTHER TURN

YOU CONSERVE ENERGY BY USING APPLIANCES ONLY IN THE EVENING AND TURNING OFF LIGHTS WHEN NOT IN USE! TAKE ANOTHER TURN

YOU FAIL TO RECYCLE YOUR TRASH!
GO BACK 3 SPACES

YOU WROTE GRAFFITI ON A NEIGHBOR-HOOD WALL!!!
LOSE A TURN

YOU LITTERED!
GO BACK 3 SPACES

YOU WASTED WATER BY OVER WATERING YOUR LAWN!
GO BACK 2 SPACES

YOU BURN LEAVES IN YOUR BACK YARD INSTEAD OF RECYCLING THEM IN YOUR GARDEN!
GO BACK 1 SPACE

YOU WASTE GASO-LINE BY ALWAYS USING YOUR CAR INSTEAD OF PUBLIC TRANSPORTATION!
GO BACK 1 SPACE

YOU POURED INSECTICIDE DOWN THE DRAIN!
LOSE A TURN

YOU WASTE ELEC-TRICITY AND POWER BY USING APPLI-ANCES DURING PEAK HOURS.
GO BACK 2 SPACES

Ecology Mobile!

Each child can make his or her own Ecology Mobile by cutting these pattern pieces from colored construction paper. (They may want to mount the finished pieces on poster board for added durability.)

TAKE CARE OF OUR EARTH

Children can list their own ideas about saving the planet on the back of each pattern piece.

95

Ecology   Button

Member of the

ECOLOGY

CLUB

BASEBALL

BASEBALL ACTIVITIES!

BASEBALL CHARACTER

BATTER UP BASEBALL BOARD GAME

BASEBALL BULLETIN BOARDS!

CREATIVE WRITING BASEBALLS!

BASEBALL ACTIVITIES!

BASEBALL

A baseball game is so much fun!
Hit the ball and then you run.
First base, second and on to third,
The ball you hit flies like a bird.

As you quickly round the bases,
People watch with anxious faces.
People watching smile and shout,
"Run to home before you're out!"

Slide into home, you can, you must,
Never mind the dirt and dust.
"You made it!" People cheer so loud!
The team is glad and aren't you proud!

BASEBALL "DREAM TEAMS"

Divide the class into three or four groups. Ask each group to cooperatively work together to create a "Baseball Team." Instruct the groups to select a team name, mascot, logo, uniform design, team song, etc. Students can draw pictures of their team and post them on the class board after reporting their efforts to the class.

BASEBALL BINGO!

This game offers an exciting way to introduce students to baseball vocabulary words. Give each child a copy of the bingo words listed below or write the words on the chalkboard. Ask students to write any 24 words on his or her bingo cards. Use the same directions you might use for regular bingo.

(Students might like to use some of these words in a creative writing assignment.)

BASEBALL	CENTER FIELD	DOUBLE	KNUCKLE BALL
BAT	LEFT FIELD	TRIPLE	CURVE BALL
MITT	COACH	HOME RUN	POP FLY
PITCHER	BATTER	OUT	BUNT
CATCHER	STRIKE	STEAL	WALK
1ST BASE	BALL	SLIDE	CROWD
2ND BASE	RUNS	SAFE	FANS
3RD BASE	INNINGS	HOME	STADIUM
SHORTSTOP	SCORE	FAST BALL	GAME
RIGHT FIELD	SINGLE	SLOW BALL	SERIES

Baseball Character!

Cut this cute baseball character from index paper. Color, cut out and fold. Attach the baseball bat to his right hand and stand on a table for a decoration.

Matching Baseballs and Mitts!

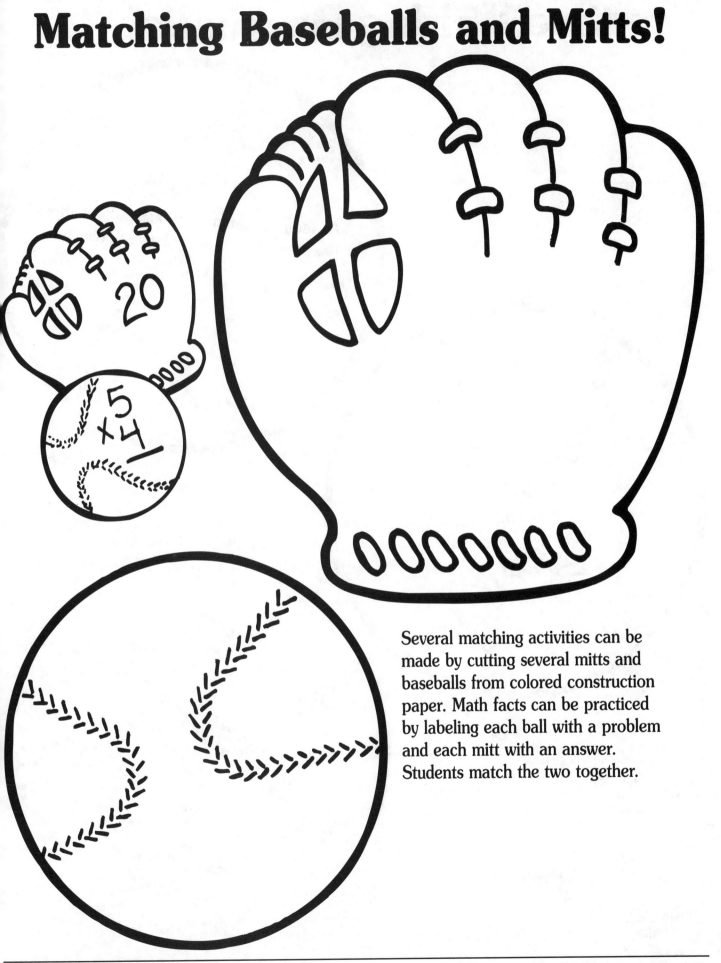

Several matching activities can be made by cutting several mitts and baseballs from colored construction paper. Math facts can be practiced by labeling each ball with a problem and each mitt with an answer. Students match the two together.

TF1604 Summer Idea Book

Creative Writing Baseballs!

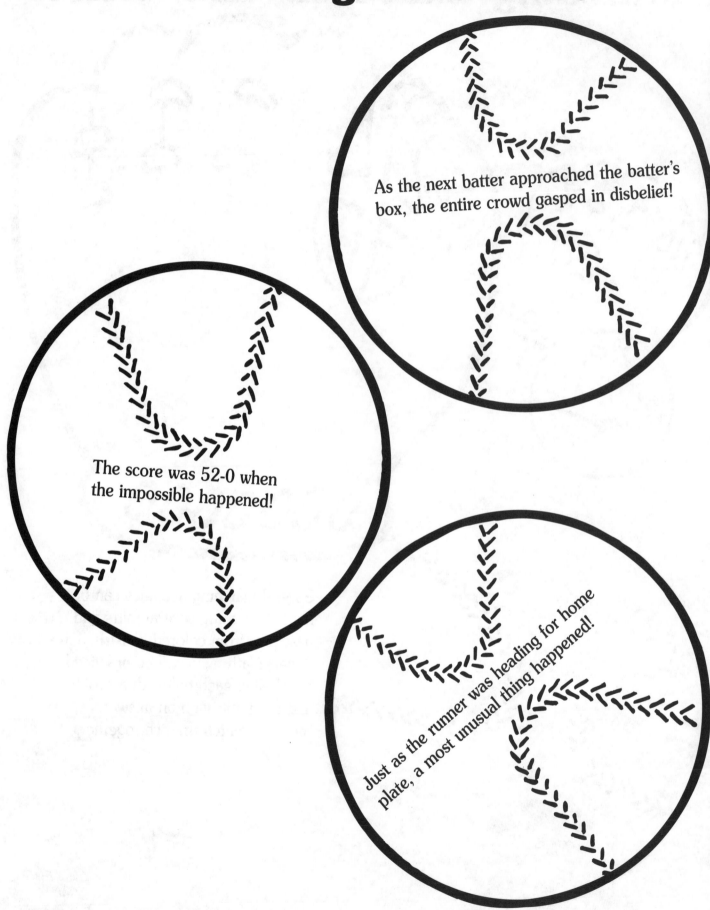

As the next batter approached the batter's box, the entire crowd gasped in disbelief!

The score was 52-0 when the impossible happened!

Just as the runner was heading for home plate, a most unusual thing happened!

TF1604 Summer Idea Book

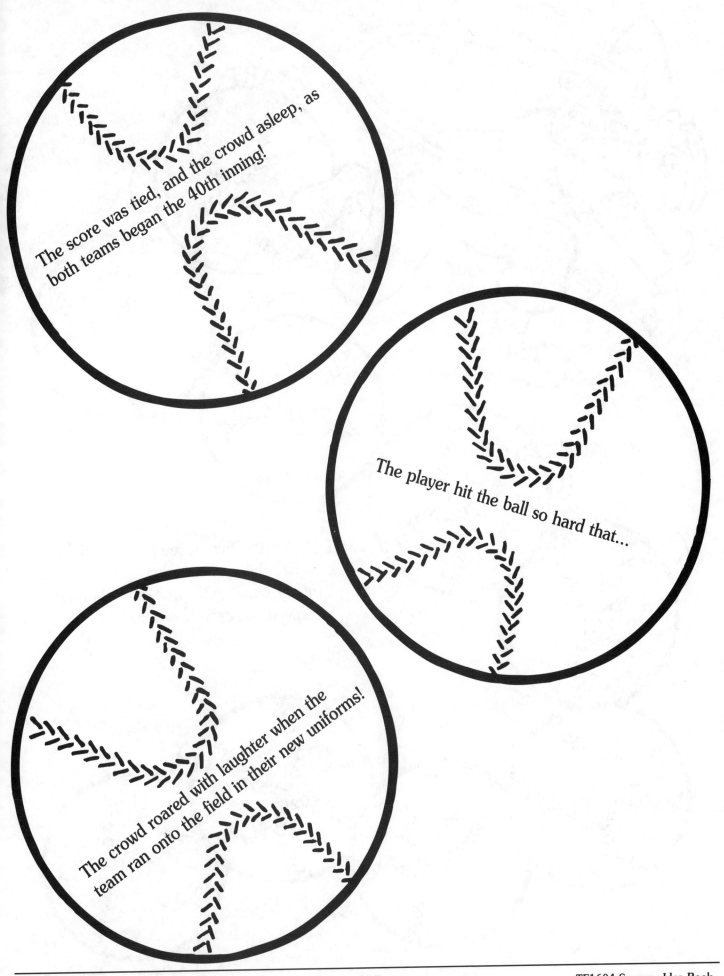

The score was tied, and the crowd asleep, as both teams began the 40th inning!

The player hit the ball so hard that...

The crowd roared with laughter when the team ran onto the field in their new uniforms!

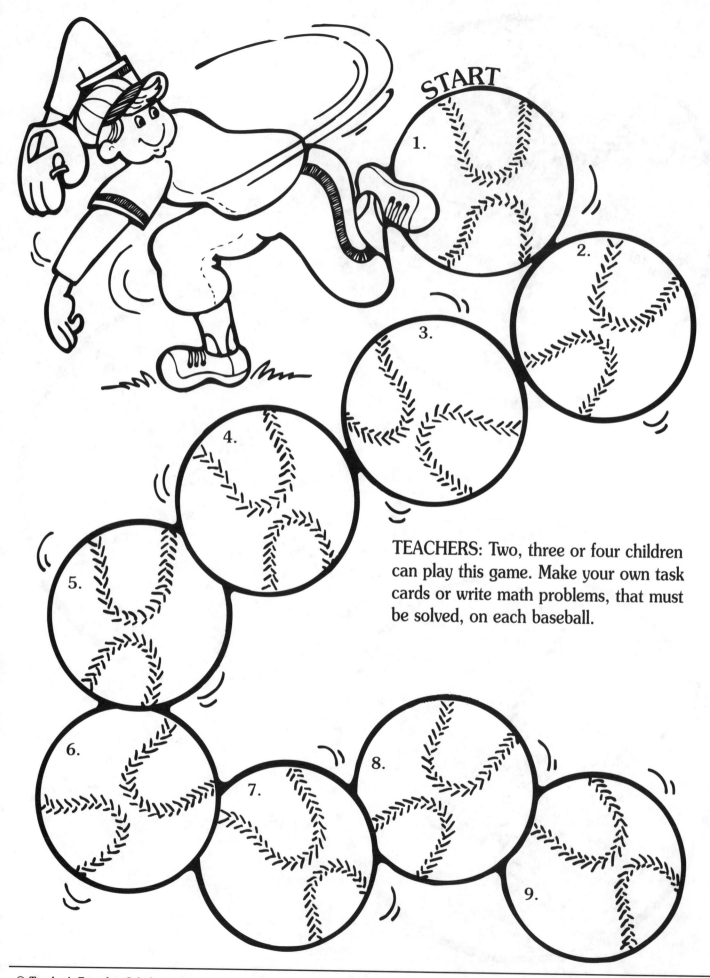

START

1.

2.

3.

4.

5.

6.

7.

8.

9.

TEACHERS: Two, three or four children can play this game. Make your own task cards or write math problems, that must be solved, on each baseball.

TF1604 Summer Idea Book

BATTER UP BASEBALL!

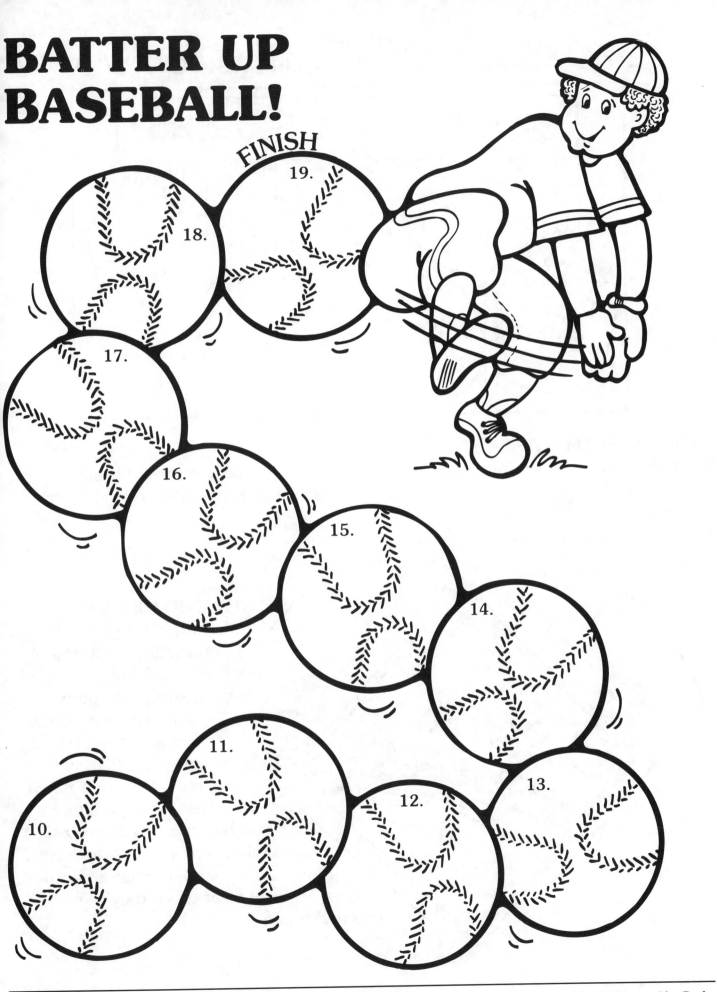

BASEBALL BULLETIN BOARDS!

GRAND SLAM STORIES!
Children will love writing creative sport stories using these mitt and baseball booklets. Arrange the booklets on the class board with the title, "Grand Slam Stories!"

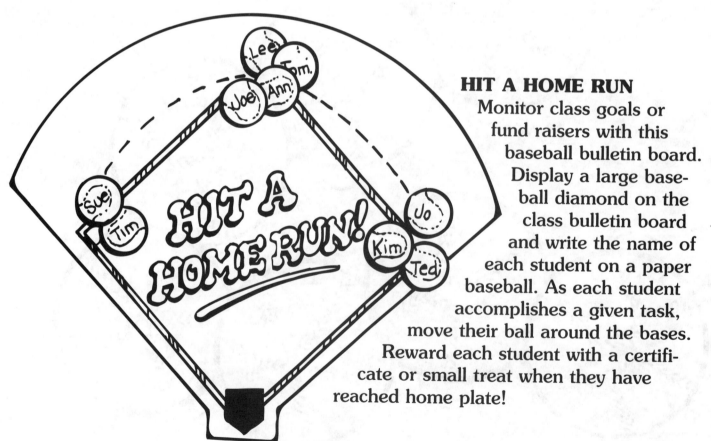

HIT A HOME RUN
Monitor class goals or fund raisers with this baseball bulletin board. Display a large baseball diamond on the class bulletin board and write the name of each student on a paper baseball. As each student accomplishes a given task, move their ball around the bases. Reward each student with a certificate or small treat when they have reached home plate!

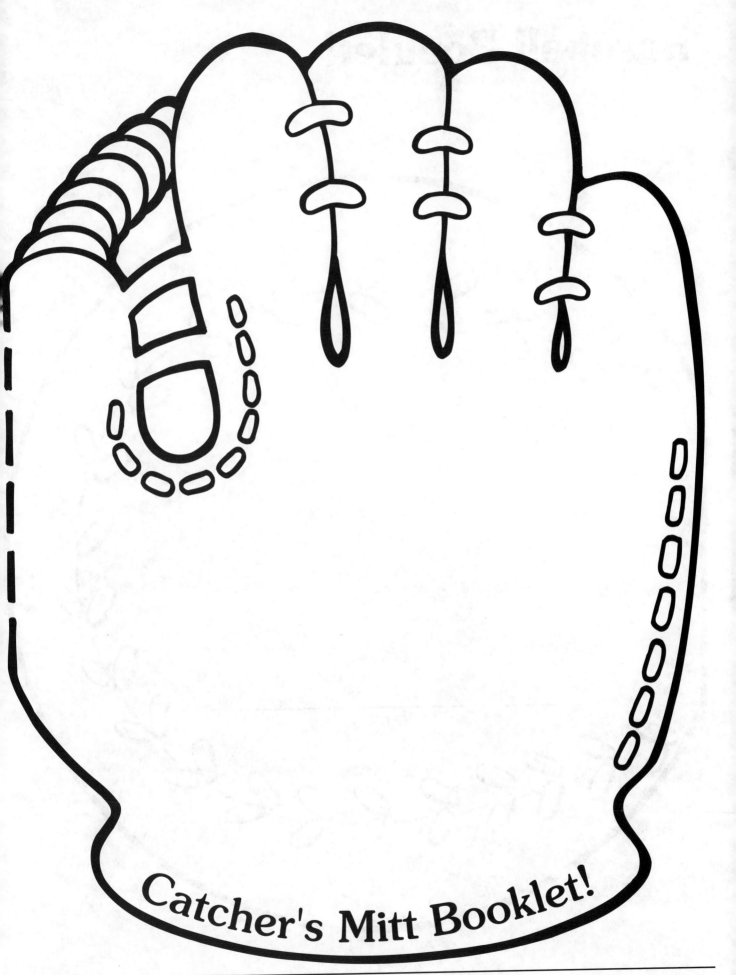

Catcher's Mitt Booklet!

 TF1604 Summer Idea Book

Baseball Booklet!

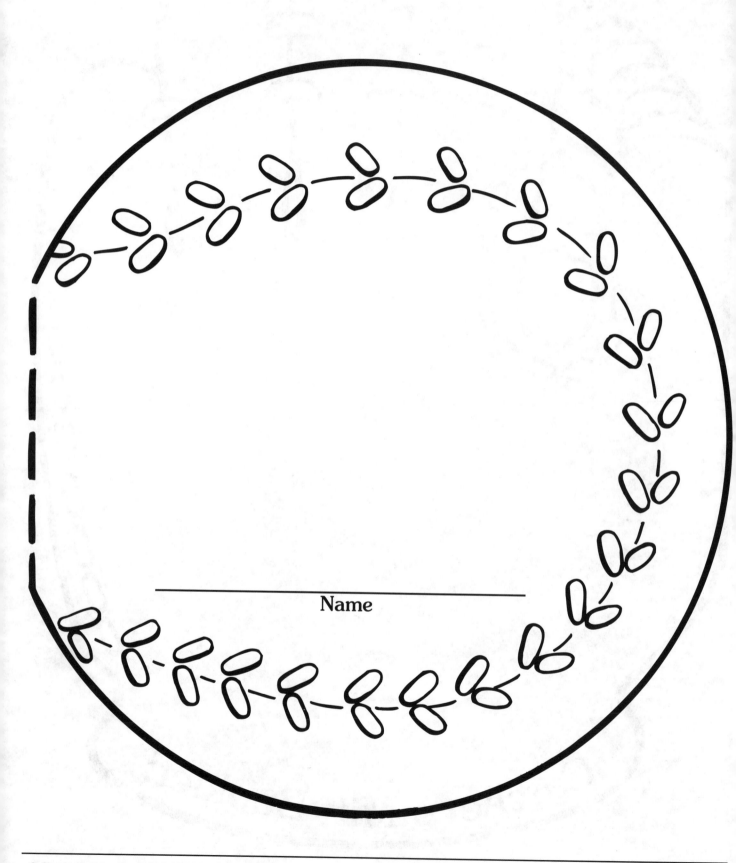

Name _____

Baseball
Characters!

TF1604 Summer Idea Book

112